Joaquin Miller

In classic shades, and other poems

Joaquin Miller

In classic shades, and other poems

ISBN/EAN: 9783743328365

Manufactured in Europe, USA, Canada, Australia, Japa

Cover: Foto ©ninafisch / pixelio.de

Manufactured and distributed by brebook publishing software (www.brebook.com)

Joaquin Miller

In classic shades, and other poems

CONTENTS.

	PAGE.
After the Battle	90
After the War	93
A Christmas Eve in the Palm Land	21
A Dead Carpenter	113
A Nubian Face on the Nile	56
A. T Stewart	105
Back to the Golden Gate	115
By the Balboa Seas	74
By the Great River	98
By the Lower Mississippi	83
By the Pacific Ocean	97
California's Christmas	67
Comanche	24
Coming	72
Custer	52
Dead in the Long, Strong Grass	119
Dedication to Juanita	4
Down the Mississippi	54
Drowned	86
Finale	127
Garfield	124
Grant at Shiloh	100
Her Picture	84
Horace Greeley's Drive	145
In Classic Shades	131
Juanita	7
La Exposicion	55
La Notte	66
Lincoln Park	58
Magnolia Blossoms	60
Manitoba	61
Montgomery at Quebec	59
My Country	91
My Last Day with Mr. Longfellow	122
Newport News	70
Olive	33
Our Heroes of To-Day	78
Outside of Church	53
Peter Cooper	104
Quebec	118
Riel, the Rebel	19
Saratoga and the Psalmist	153
Sierra	118
The Battle-Flag at Shenandoah	34
The Birth of California's Arbor Day	102

CONTENTS.

Title	PAGE
The Fortunate Isles	116
The Gold that Grew by Shasta Town	41
The Larger College	106
The Lost Regiment	37
The Lost Boy Regiments	81
The New President	63
The Poem by the Potomac	110
The River of Rest	65
The Sioux Chief's Daughter	46
The Size of Souls	118
The Soldiers' Home, Washington	28
The True Poet	71
The World is a Better World	57
That Faithful Wife of Idaho	149
That Gentleman from Boston Town	135
Those Perilous Spanish Eyes	69
"To Die for the Country"	75
To Mount Shasta	126
To Russia	15
To Rachel in Russia	17
To the Czar	11
Twilight on Oakland Heights	101
William Brown of Oregon	140

JUANITA.

You will come my bird, bonnita?
   Come! For I by steep and stone
Have built such nest for you, Juanita,
   As not eagle bird hath known.

Rugged! Rugged as Parnassus!
   Rude, as all roads I have trod—
Yet are steeps and stone-strown passes
   Smooth o'er head, and nearest God.

Here black thunders of my canyon
   Shake its walls in Titan wars!
Here white sea-born clouds companion
   With such peaks as know the stars!

Here madrona, manzineta—
   Here the snarling chaparral
House and hang o'er steeps, Juanita,
   Where the gaunt wolf loved to dwell!

JUANITA.

Dear, I took these trackless masses
   Fresh from Him who fashioned them;
Wrought in rock, and hewed fair passes,
   Flower set, as sets a gem.

Aye, I built in woe. God willed it;
   Woe that passeth ghosts of guilt.
Yet I built as His birds builded—
   Builded singing as I built.

All is finished! Roads of flowers
   Wait your loyal little feet.
All completed? Nay, the hours
   Till you come are incomplete.

Steep below me lies the valley,
   Deep below me lies the town,
Where great sea-ships ride and rally,
   And the world walks up and down.

O, the sea of lights for streaming
   When the thousand flags are furled—
When the gleaming bay lies dreaming
   As it duplicates the world!

You will come my dearest, truest?
  Come my sovereign queen of ten;
My blue skies will then be bluest;
  My white rose be whitest then:

Then the song! Ah, then the sabre
  Flashing up the walls of night!
Hate of wrong and love of neighbor—
  Rhymes of battle for the Right!

TO THE CZAR.

Down from her high estate she stept,
  A maiden, gently born,
And by the icy Volga kept
  Sad watch, and waited morn;
And peasants say that where she slept
  The new moon dipt her horn.
    Yet on and on, through shoreless snows,
      Far tow'rd the bleak north pole,
    The foulest wrong the good God knows
      Rolled as dark rivers roll.
    While never once for all their woes
      Upspake your ruthless soul.

She toiled, she taught the peasant, taught
  The dark-eyed Tartar. He,
Illumined with her lofty thought,
  Rose up and sought to be,
What God at the creation wrought,
  A man! God-like and free.

TO THE CZAR.

Yet still before him yawned the black
  Siberian mines!   And oh,
The knout upon the bare white back!
  The blood upon the snow!
The gaunt wolves, close upon the track,
  Fought o'er the fallen so!

And this that one might wear a crown
  Snatched from a strangled sire!
And this that two might mock or frown,
  From high thrones climbing higher—
From where the Parricide looked down
  With harlot in desire!

Yet on, beneath the great north star,
  Like some lost, living thing,
That long dread line stretched, black and far
  Till buried by death's wing!
And great men praised the goodly Czar—
  But God sat pitying.

*   *   *   *   *   *

A storm burst forth!   From out the storm
  The clean, red lightning leapt,
And lo, a prostrate royal form . . . .
  And Alexander slept!
Down through the snow, all smoking warm,
  Like any blood, his crept.

TO THE CZAR.

Yea, one lay dead, for millions dead!
  One red spot in the snow
For one long damning line of red,
  Where exiles endless go—
The babe at breast, the mother's head
  Bowed down, and dying so!

And did a woman do this deed?
  Then build her scaffold high,
That all may on her forehead read
  The martyr's right to die!
Ring Cossack round on royal steed!
  Now lift her to the sky!
    But see! From out the black hood shines
      A light few look upon!
    Lorn exiles, see, from dark, deep mines,
      A star at burst of dawn! . . . .
    A thud! A creak of hangman's lines!—
      A frail shape jerked and drawn! . . . . .

   *   *   *   *   *   *

The Czar is dead; the woman dead,
  About her neck a cord.
In God's house rests his royal head—
  Hers in a place abhorred:
Yet I had rather have her bed
  Than thine, most royal lord!

Yea, rather be that woman dead,
 Than thee, dead-living Czar,
To hide in dread, with both hands red,
 Behind great bolt and bar. . .
You may control to the North Pole,
 But God still guides His star.

TO RUSSIA.

"Where wast thou when I laid the foundations of the earth?"
—*Bible.*

Who tamed your lawless Tartar blood?
   What David bearded in her den
   The Russian bear in ages when
You strode your black; unbridled stud,
A skin-clad savage of your steeps?
Why, one who now sits low and weeps,
Why one who now wails out to you—
The Jew, the homeless, hated Jew.

Who girt the thews of your young prime
   And bound your fierce divided force?
   Why, who but Moses shaped your course
United down the grooves of time?
Your mighty millions all to-day
The hated, homeless Jews obey.
Who taught all poetry to you?
The Jew, the hated, homeless Jew.

Who taught you tender Bible tales
   Of honey-lands, of milk and wine?
   Of happy, peaceful Palestine?
Of Jordan's holy harvest-vales?
Who gave the patient Christ? I say,
Who gave your Christian creed? Yea, yea,
Who gave your very God to you?
Your Jew! Your Jew! Your hated Jew!

TO RACHEL IN RUSSIA.

"To bring them unto a good land and a large; unto a land flowing with milk and honey."

O Thou, whose patient, peaceful blood
Paints Sharon's roses on thy cheek,
And down thy breasts plays hide and seek,
Six thousand years a stainless flood,
Rise up and set thy sad face hence.
Rise up and come where Freedom waits
Within these white, wide ocean-gates
To give thee God's inheritance;
To bind thy wounds in this despair;
To braid thy long, strong, loosened hair.

O Rachel, weeping where the flood
Of icy Volga grinds and flows
Against his banks of blood-red snows—
White banks made red with children's blood—
Lift up thy head, be comforted;
For, as thou didst on manna feed,

When Russia roamed a bear in deed,
And on her own foul essence fed,
So shalt thou flourish as a tree
When Russ and Cossack shall not be.

Then come where yellow harvests swell ·
Forsake the savage land of snows ;
Forget the brutal Russian's blows ;
And come where Kings of Conscience dwell.
Oh come, Rebecca to the well !
The voice of Rachel shall be sweet,
The Gleaner rest safe at the feet
Of one who loves her ; and the spell
Of Peace that blesses Paradise
Shall kiss thy large and lonely eyes.

RIEL: THE REBEL.

He died at dawn in the land of snows,
  A priest at the left, a priest at the right;
The doomed man praying for his pitiless foes,
  And each priest holding a low dim lamp,
  To pray for the soul of the dying.
    But Windsor Castle was far away;
    And Windsor Castle was never so gay
  With her gorgeous banners flying!

The hero was hung in the windy dawn—
  'Twas splendidly done, the telegraph said;
A creak of the neck, then the shoulders drawn;
  A heave of the breast—and the man hung dead,
  And, oh! never such valiant dying!
    While Windsor Castle was far away
    With its fops and fools on that windy day,
  And its thousand banners flying!

Some starving babes where a stark stream flows
  'Twixt windy banks by an Indian town,
A frenzied mother in the freezing snows,
  While softly the pitying snow came down

To cover the dead and the dying.
    But Windsor Castle was gorgeous and gay
    With lion banners that windy day—
With lying banners flying.

A CHRISTMAS EVE IN THE PALM LAND.

Their priests are many, for many their sins,
　Their sins are many, for their land is fair;
The perfumed waves and the perfumed winds,
　The cocoa-palms and the perfumed air;
　　The proud old Dons, so poor and so proud,
　　So poor their ghosts can scarce wear a shroud—
This town of Columbus has priests and prayer;
　　And great bells pealing in the palm land.

A proud Spanish Don lies shriven and dead;
　The cross on his breast, a priest at his prayer:
His slave at his feet, his son at his head—
　A slave's white face in a mantle of hair;
　　A slave's white face, why, a face as white,
　　As white as that dead man's face this night—
This town of Columbus can pray for the dead;
　　And great bells booming in the palm land.

The moon hangs white up at heaven's white door,
　Quite dead in the isle of the great, warm seas
Lies the old proud Don, so proud and so poor,
　And two quite close by the bed on their knees;

The slave at his feet, the son at his head,
And both in tears for the proud man dead—
This town of Columbus has tears if you please;
   And great bells pealing in the palm land.

Aye, both are in tears; for a child might trace
  In the face of the slave, as the face of the son,
The same proud look of the dead man's face—
  The beauty of one; and the valor of one—
    The slave at his feet, the son at his head,
    This night of Christ, where the Don lies dead—
This town of Columbus, this land of the sun
    Keeps great bells clanging in the palm land.

The slave is so fair, and so wonderful fair!
  A statue stepped out from some temple of old;
Why, you could entwine your two hands in her hair,
  Nor yet could encompass its ample, dark fold.
   And oh, that pitiful, upturned face;
   Her master lies dead—she knows her place.
This town of Columbus has hundreds at prayer,
   And great bells booming in the palm land.

The proud Don dead, and this son his heir;
  This slave his fortune. Now what shall he do?
Why, what should he do? or what should he care,
  Save only to cherish a pride as true?—

    To hide his shame as the good priests hide
    Black sins confessed when the damned have died.
This town of Columbus has pride with her prayer—
    And great bells pealing in the palm land !

Lo, Christ's own hour in the argent seas,
    And she, his sister, his own born slave !
His secret is safe; just master and she;
    These two, and the dead at the door of the grave. . .
    And death, whatever our other friends do,
    Why, death, my friend, is a friend most true—
This town of Columbus keeps pride and keeps prayer,
    And great bells booming in the palm land.

COMANCHE.

A blazing home, a blood-soaked hearth;
   Fair woman's hair with blood upon!
That Ishmaelite of all the earth
   Has like a cyclone, come and gone —
His feet are as the blighting dearth;
   His hands are daggers drawn.

"To horse! to horse!" the rangers shout,
   And red revenge is on his track!
The black-haired Bedouin en route
   Looks like a long, bent line of black.
He does not halt nor turn about;
   He scorns to once look back.

But on! right on that line of black,
   Across the snow-white, sand-sown pass;
The bearded rangers on their track
   Bear thirsty sabres bright as glass.
Yet not one red man there looks back;
   His nerves are braided brass.

  *   *   *   *   *   *

At last, at last, their mountain came
   To clasp its children in their flight !
Up, up from out the sands of flame
   They clambered, bleeding, to their height ;
This savage summit, now so tame,
   Their lone star, that dread night !

"Huzzah ! Dismount ! " the captain cried.
   " Huzzah ! the rovers cease to roam !
The river keeps yon farther side,
   A roaring cataract of foam.
They die, they die for those who died
   Last night by hearth and home ! "

His men stood still beneath the steep;
   The high, still moon stood like a nun.
The horses stood as willows weep;
   Their weary heads drooped every one.
But no man there had thought of sleep;
   Each waited for the sun.

Vast nun-white moon ! Her silver rill
   Of snow-white peace she ceaseless poured;
The rock-built battlement grew still,
   The deep-down river roared and roared.
But each man there with iron will
   Leaned silent on his sword.

Hark! See what light starts from the steep!
　And hear, ah, hear that piercing sound.
It is their lorn death-song they keep
　In solemn and majestic round.
The red fox of these deserts deep
　At last is run to ground.

*　　*　　*　　*　　*　　*　　*　　*　　*

Oh, it was weird,—that wild, pent horde!
　Their death-lights, their death-wails each one.
The river in sad chorus roared
　And boomed like some great funeral gun.
The while each ranger nursed his sword
　And waited for the sun.

Then sudden star-tipped mountains topt
　With flame beyond! And watch-fires ran
To where white peaks high heaven propt;
　And star and light left scarce a span.
Why none could say where death-lights stopt
　Or where red stars began!

And then the far, wild wails that came
　In tremulous and pitying flight
From star-lit peak and peak of flame!
　Wails that had lost their way that night
And knocked at each heart's door to claim
　Protection in their flight.

O, chu-lu-le!   O, chu-lu-lo!
   A thousand red hands reached in air.
O, chu-lu-le!   O, chu-lu-lo!
   When midnight housed in midnight hair,
O, chu-lu-le!   O, chu-lu-lo!
   Their one last wailing prayer.

And all night long, nude Rachels poured
   Melodious pity one by one
From mountain top.   The river roared
   Sad requiem for his braves undone.
The while each ranger nursed his sword
   And waited for the sun.

THE SOLDIERS' HOME, WASHINGTON.

The monument, tipped with electric fire,
    Blazed high in a halo of light below
My low cabin door in the hills that inspire;
    And the dome of the Capitol gleamed like snow
In a glory of light, as higher and higher
    This wondrous creation of man was sent
    To challenge the lights of the firmament.

A tall man, tawny and spare as bone,
    With battered old hat and with feet half bare,
With the air of a soldier that was all his own—
    Aye, something more than a soldier's air—
    Came clutching a staff, with a face like stone;
    Limped in through my gate—and I thought to beg—
    Tight clutching a staff, slow dragging a leg.

The moon, like a sharp-drawn cimeter,
    Kept peace in Heaven. All earth lay still.
Some sentinel stars stood watch afar,
    Some crickets kept clanging along the hill,
As the tall, stern relic of blood and war
    Limped in, and, with hand up to brow half raised,
    Limped up, looked out, as one dazed or crazed.

His gaunt face pleading for food and rest,
  His set lips white as a tale of shame,
His black coat tight to a shirtless breast,
  His black eyes burning in mine-like flame;
  But never a word from his set lips came
  As he whipped in line his battered old leg
  And his knees made mouths as if to beg.

Aye! black were his eyes; but doubtful and dim
  Their vision of beautiful earth, I think.
And I doubt if the distant, dear worlds to him
  Were growing brighter as he neared the brink
Of dolorous seas where phantom ships swim.
  For his face was as hard as the hard, thin hand
  That clutched that staff like an iron band.

"Sir, I am a soldier!" The battered old hat
  Stood up as he spake, like to one on parade—
Stood taller and braver as he spake out that—
  And the tattered old coat, that was tightly laid
To the battered old breast, looked so trim thereat
  That I knew the mouths of the battered old leg
  That had opened wide were not made to beg.

" I have wandered and wandered this twenty year:
  Searched up and down for my regiments.
Have they gone to that field where no foes appear?

Have they pitched in Heaven their cloud-white
 tents?
Or, tell me, my friend, shall I find them here
 On the hill beyond, at the Soldiers' Home,
 Where the weary soldiers have ceased to roam?

"Aye, I am a soldier and a brigadier.
 Is this the way to the Soldiers' Home?
There is plenty and rest for us all, I hear,
 And a bugler, bidding us cease to roam,
Rides over the hill the livelong year—
 Rides calling and calling the brave to come
And rest and rest in that Soldiers' Home.

"Is this the way? I wandered in here
 Just as one will at the close of day.
Aye, I am a soldier and a brigadier!
 Now, the Soldiers' Home, sir. Is this the way?
I have wandered and wandered this twenty year,
 Seeking some trace of my regiments
 Sabered and riddled and torn to rents.

"Aye, I am a soldier and a brigadier!
 A battered old soldier in the dusk of his day;
But you don't seem to heed, or you don't seem to hear,
 Though, meek as I may, I ask for the way

To the Soldiers' Home, which must be quite near.
   Yet under your oaks, in your easy chair,
   You sit and you sit, and you stare and you stare.

"What battle? What deeds did I do in the fight?
   Why, sir, I have seen green fields turn as red
As yonder red town in that marvelous light!
   Then the great blazing guns! Then the ghastly
     white dead—
   But, tell me, I faint, I must cease to roam!
This battered leg aches! Then this sabered old
     head—
   Is—*is* this the way to the Soldiers' Home?

"Why, I hear men say 't is a Paradise
   On the green oak hills by the great red town;
That many old comrades shall meet my eyes;
   That a tasseled young trooper rides up and rides
     down,
With bugle-horn blowing to the still blue skies,
   Calling and calling to rest and to stay
   In that Soldiers' Home. Sir, is this the way?

"My leg is so lame! Then this sabered old head—
   Ah! pardon me, sir, I never complain;
But the road is so rough, as I just now said;
   And then there is something that troubles my brain.

It makes the light dance from yon Capitol's dome;
It makes the road dim as I doubtfully tread.
But is this the way to the Soldier's Home?

"From the first to the last in that desperate war—
  Why, I did my part. If I did not fall,
A hairs-breadth measure of this skull-bone scar
  Was all that was wanting; and then this ball—
But what cared I? Ah! better by far
  Have a sabered old head and a shattered old knee
  To the end, than not had the praise of Lee—

"What! What do I hear? No home there for me?
  Why, I heard men say that the war was at end!
Oh, my head swims so; and I scarce can see!
  But a soldier's a soldier, I think, my friend,
Wherever that soldier may chance to be!
  And wherever a soldier may chance to roam,
  Why, a Soldiers' Home is a soldier's home!"

He turned as to go; but he sank to the grass;
  And I lifted my face to the firmament;
For I saw a sentinel white star pass,
  Leading the way the old soldier went.
And the light shone bright from the Capitol's dome,
  Brighter indeed from the monument,
Lighting his way to the Soldiers' Home.

OLIVE.

Dove-borne symbol, olive bough;
  Dove-hued sign from God to men,
As if still the dove and thou
  Kept companionship as then.

Dove-hued, holy branch of peace,
  Antique, all-enduring tree;
Deluge and the floods surcease—
  Deluge and Gethsemane.

THE BATTLE FLAG AT SHENANDOAH.

The tented field wore a wrinkled frown,
And the emptied church from the hill looked down
On the emptied road and the emptied town,
    That summer Sunday morning.

And here was the blue, and there was the gray;
And a wide green valley rolled away
Between where the battling armies lay,
    That sacred Sunday morning.

And Custer sat, with impatient will,
His restless steed, 'mid his troopers still,
As he watched with glass from the oak-set hill,
    That silent Sunday morning.

Then fast he began to chafe and fret;
"There's a battle flag on a bayonet
Too close to my own true soldiers set
    For peace this Sunday morning!"

"Ride over, some one," he haughtily said,
"And bring it to me !   Why, in bars blood red
And in stars I will stain it, and overhead
      Will flaunt it this Sunday morning !"

Then a West-born lad, pale-faced and slim,
Rode out, and touching his cap to him,
Swept down, as swift as the swallows swim,
      That anxious Sunday morning

On, on through the valley ! up, up, anywhere !
That pale-faced lad like a bird through the air
Kept on till he climbed to the banner there
      That bravest Sunday morning !

And he caught up the flag, and around his waist
He wound it tight, and he turned in haste,
And swift his perilous route retraced
      That daring Sunday morning.

All honor and praise to the trusty steed !
Ah ! boy, and banner, and all God speed !
God's pity for you in your hour of need
      This deadly Sunday morning.

O, deadly shot! and O, shower of lead!
O, iron rain on the brave, bare head!
Why, even the leaves from the trees fall dead
    This dreadful Sunday morning!

But he gains the oaks! Men cheer in their might!
Brave Custer is weeping in his delight!
Why, he is embracing the boy outright
    This glorious Sunday morning!

But, soft! Not a word has the pale boy said.
He unwinds the flag. It is starred, striped, red
With his heart's best blood; and he falls down dead,
    In God's still Sunday morning.

So, wrap his flag to his soldier's breast;
Into stars and stripes it is stained, and blest;
And under the oaks let him rest and rest
    Till God's great Sunday morning.

THE LOST REGIMENT.

[In a pretty little village in Louisiana, destroyed by shells toward the end of the war, on a bayou back from the river, a great number of very old men had been left by their sons and grandsons, while they went to the war. And these old men, many of them veterans of other wars, formed themselves into a regiment, made for themselves uniforms, picked up old flintlock guns, even mounted a rusty old cannon, and so prepared to go to battle if ever the war came within their reach. Toward the close of the war some gunboats came down the river shelling the shore. The old men heard the firing, and, gathering together, they set out with their old muskets and rusty old cannon to try to reach the river over the corduroy road through the cypress swamp. They marched out right merrily that hot day, shouting and bantering to encourage each other, the dim fires of their old eyes burning with desire of battle, although not one of them was young enough to stand erect And they never came back any more. The shells from the gunboats set the dense and sultry woods on fire. The old men were shut in by the flames—the gray beards and the gray moss and the gray smoke together.]

THE dying land cried; they heard her death-call,
    These bent, old men stopped, listened intent;
Then rusty old muskets rushed down from the wall,
    And squirrel-guns gleamed in that regiment,
And grandsires marched, old muskets in hand—
The last men left in the whole Southland.

The gray grandsires! They were seen to reel,
  Their rusty old muskets a wearisome load;
They marched, scarce tall as the cannon's wheel,
  Marched merrily on up the corduroy road;
These gray old boys, all broken and bent,
Marched out, the gallant last regiment.

But oh! that march through the cypress-trees,
  When zest and excitement had died away!
That desolate march through the marsh to the
      knees—
These gray grandsires all broken and bent—
The gray moss mantling the regiment.

The gray bent men and the mosses gray;
  The dull dead gray of the uniform!
The dull dead skies, like to lead that day,
  Dull, dead, heavy and deathly warm!
Oh, what meant more than the cypress meant,
With its mournful moss, to that regiment?

That deadly march through the marshes deep!
  That sultry day and the deeds in vain!
The rest on the cypress roots, the sleep—
  The sleeping never to rise again!
The rust on the guns; the rust and the rent—
That dying and desolate regiment!

THE LOST REGIMENT.

The muskets left leaning against the trees,
  The cannon wheels clogged from the moss o'erhead,
The cypress-trees bending on obstin'ate knees
  As gray men kneeled by the gray men dead!
A lone bird rising, long legged and gray,
Slow rising and rising and drifting away.

The dank dead mosses gave back no sound,
  The drums lay silent as the drummers there;
The sultry stillness was so profound
  You might have heard an unuttered prayer;
And ever and ever and far away,
Kept drifting that desolate bird in gray.

The long gray shrouds of that cypress wood,
  Like veils that sweep where the gray nuns weep—
That cypress moss o'er the dankness deep,
  Why, the cypress roots they were running blood;
And to right and to left lay an old man dead—
A mourning cypress set foot and head.

'T was man hunting man in the wilderness there;
  'T was man hunting man and hunting to slay;
But nothing was found but death that day,
  And possibly God in that poisonous air;
And possibly God—and that bird in gray
Slow rising and rising and drifting away.

Now down in the swamp where the gray men fell
    The fireflies volley and volley at night,
And black men belated are heard to tell
    Of the ghosts in gray in a mimic fight—
Of the ghosts of the gallant old men in gray
Who silently died in the swamp that day.

THE GOLD THAT GREW BY SHASTA TOWN.

From Shasta town to Redding town
    The ground is torn by miners dead;
    The manzanita, rank and red,
Drops dusty berries up and down
    Their grass-grown trails. Their silent mines
    Are wrapped in chapparal and vines;
Yet one gray miner still sits down
'Twixt Redding and sweet Shasta town.

The quail pipes pleasantly. The hare
    Leaps careless o'er the golden oat
    That grows below the water moat;
The lizard basks in sunlight there.
The brown hawk swims the perfumed air
    Unfrightened through the livelong day;
And now and then a curious bear
    Comes shuffling down the ditch by night,
    And leaves some wide, long tracks in clay
    So human-like, so stealthy light;
Where one lone cabin still stoops down
'Twixt Redding and sweet Shasta town.

That great graveyard of hopes! of men
    Who sought for hidden veins of gold;
    Of young men suddenly grown old—
Of old men dead, despairing when
    The gold was just within their hold !
That storied land, whereon the light
    Of other days gleams faintly still ;
    Somelike the halo of a hill
That lifts above the falling night ;
    That warm, red, rich and human land,
    That flesh-red soil, that warm red sand,
Where one gray miner still sits down !
Twixt Redding and sweet Shasta town !

"I know the vein is here !" he said;
    For twenty years, for thirty years !
    While far away fell tears on tears
From wife and babe who mourned him dead.

No gold ! No gold ! And he grew old
    And crept to toil with bended head
    Amid a graveyard of his dead,
Still seeking for that vein of gold.

Then lo, came laughing down the years
A sweet grandchild ! Between his tears

He laughed. He set her by the door
   The while he toiled; his day's toil o'er
He held her chubby cheeks between
   His hard palms, laughed; and laughing cried.
You should have seen, have heard and seen
   His boyish joy, his stout old pride,
When toil was done and he sat down
At night, below sweet Shasta town!

At last his strength was gone. "No more!
   I mine no more. I plant me now
A vine and fig-tree; worn and old,
   I seek no more my vein of gold.
But, oh, I sigh to give it o'er;
   These thirty years of toil! somehow
It seems so hard; but now, no more."
   And so the old man set him down
To plant, by pleasant Shasta town.
And it was pleasant; piped the quail
   The full year through. The chipmunk stole,
His whiskered nose and tossy tail
   Full buried in the sugar-bowl.

And purple grapes and grapes of gold
   Swung sweet as milk. While orange-trees
   Grew brown with laden honey-bees.

Oh! it was pleasant up and down
That vine-set hill of Shasta town!
   *   *   *   *   *   *

And then that cloud-burst came! Ah, me!
  That torn ditch there! The mellow land
  Rolled seaward like a rope of sand,
Nor left one leafy vine or tree
Of all that Eden nestling down
Below that moat by Shasta town!
   *   *   *   *   *   *

The old man sat his cabin's sill,
  His gray head bowed upon his knee;
    The child went forth, sang pleasantly,
      Where burst the ditch the day before,
And picked some pebbles from the hill.
    The old man moaned, moaned o'er and o'er:
" My babe is dowerless, and I
Must fold my helpless hands and die!
  Ah, me! What curse comes ever down
  On me and mine at Shasta town!"

" Good Grandpa, see!" the glad child said,
  And so leaned softly to his side,—
Laid her gold head to his gray head,
  And merry voiced and cheery cried,

" Good Grandpa : do not weep, but see !
　I've found a peck of orange seeds !
I searched the hill for vine or tree ;
　　Not one !—not even oats or weeds ;
　　But, oh ! such heaps of orange seeds !

' Come, good Grandpa ! Now once you said
　　That God is good. So this may teach
　　That we must plant each seed, and each
　　　May grow to be an orange-tree.
Now, good Grandpa, please raise your head,
　　　And please come plant the seeds with me."
　　And prattling thus, or like to this,
　　The child thrust her full hands in his.

He sprang, sprang upright as of old.
　'Tis gold ! 'tis gold ! my hidden vein !
'Tis gold for you, sweet babe, 'tis gold !
　　Yea, God is good ; we plant again ! "
　　　So one old miner still sits down
　　　By pleasant, sunlit Shasta town.

THE SIOUX CHIEF'S DAUGHTER.

Two gray hawks ride the rising blast;
Dark cloven cloud drive to and fro
By peaks pre-eminent in snow;
A sounding river rushes past,
So wild, so vortex-like, and vast.

A lone lodge tops the windy hill;
A tawny maiden, mute and still,
Stands waiting at the river's brink,
As weird and wild as you can think.
  A mighty chief is at her feet;
She does not heed him wooing so—
She hears the dark, wild waters flow;
  She waits her lover, tall and fleet,
From off the beaming hills of snow.

He comes! The grim chief springs in air—
His brawny arm, his blade is bare.

She turns; she lifts her round, brown hand;
She looks him fairly in the face;
She moves her foot a little pace

And says, with calmness and command,
"There's blood enough in this lorn land.

"But see! a test of strength and skill,
Of courage and fierce fortitude;
To breast and wrestle with the rude
And storm-born waters, now I will
Bestow you both.

" .   .   .   Stand either side!
And you, my burly chief, I know
Would choose my right. Now peer you low
Across the waters wild and wide.
See! leaning so this morn I spied
Red berries dip yon farther side.

"See, dipping, dripping in the stream!
Twin boughs of autumn berries gleam!

"Now this, brave men, shall be the test:
Plunge in the stream, bear knife in teeth
To cut yon bough for bridal wreath.
Plunge in! and he who bears him best,
And brings yon ruddy fruit to land
The first, shall have both heart and hand."

Two tawny men, tall, brown, and thewed
Like antique bronzes rarely seen,
Shot up like flame.

                She stood between
Like fixed, impassive fortitude.
Then one threw robes with sullen air,
And wound red fox-tails in his hair;
But one with face of proud delight
Entwined a crest of snowy white.

She stood between. She sudden gave
The sign and each impatient brave
Shot sudden in the sounding wave;
The startled waters gurgled round;
Their stubborn strokes kept sullen sound.

Oh, then awoke the love that slept!
Oh, then her heart beat loud and strong!
Oh, then the proud love pent up long
Broke forth in wail upon the air!
And leaning there she sobbed and wept,
With dark face mantled in her hair.

She lifts at last her leaning brow,
He nears the shore, her love! and now

The foam flies spouting from a face
That laughing lifts from out the race.

The race is won, the work is done!
She sees the kingly crest of snow;
She knows her tall, brown Idaho.
She cries aloud, she laughing cries,
And tears are streaming from her eyes:
"O splendid, kingly Idaho!
I kiss thy lifted crest of snow;

" My tall and tawny king, come back!
Come swift, O sweet! why falter so?
Come! Come! What thing has crossed your track?
I kneel to all the gods I know.
Great Spirit, what is this I dread?
Why there is blood! the wave is red!
That wrinkled chief, outstripped in race,
Dives down, and, hiding from my face,
Strikes underneath.

" .   .   .   He rises now!
Now plucks my hero's berry bough,
And lifts aloft his red fox head,
And signals he has won for me.   .   .   .
Hist, softly!   Let him come and see.

"Oh, come! my white-crowned hero, come!
Oh, come! and I will be your bride,
Despite yon chieftain's craft and might.
Come back to me! my lips are dumb,
My hands are helpless with dispair;
The hair you kissed, my long, strong hair,
Is reaching to the ruddy tide,
That you may clutch it when you come.

"How slow he buffets back the wave!
O God, he sinks! O Heaven! save
My brave, brave king! He rises! see!
Hold fast, my hero! Strike for me.
Strike straight this way! Strike firm and strong!
Hold fast your strength. It is not long—
O God, he sinks! He sinks! Is gone!

"And did I dream and do I wake?
Or did I wake and now but dream?
And what is this crawls from the stream?
Oh, here is some mad, mad mistake!
What, you! The red fox at my feet?
You first, and failing from a race?
What! You have brought me berries red?
What! You have brought your bride a wreath?
You sly red fox with wrinkled face—
That blade has blood between your teeth!

"Lie low! lie low! now I lean o'er
And clutch your red blade to the shore. . . .
Ha! ha! Take that! and that! and dream!
Ha, ha! So, through your coward throat
The full day shines! . . . Two fox-tails float
And drift and drive far down the stream.

"But what is this? What snowy crest
Climbs out the willows of the west,
All dripping from his streaming hair?
'T is he! My hero brave and fair!
His face is lifting to my face,
And who shall now dispute the race?

"The gray hawks pass, O love! and doves
O'er yonder lodge shall coo their loves.
My hands shall heal your wounded breast,
And in yon tall lodge two shall rest."

CUSTER.

    Oh, it were better dying there
    On glory's front, with trumpets' blare,
    And battle's shout blent wild about—
  The sense of sacrifice, the roar
Of war! The soul might well leap out—
The brave, white soul leap boldly out
The door of wounds, and up the stair
    Of heaven to God's open door,
While yet the knees were bent in prayer.

OUTSIDE OF CHURCH.

It seems to me a grandest thing
To save the soul from perishing
By planting it where heaven's rain
May reach and make it grow again.

It seems to me the man who leaves
    The soul to perish is as one
Who gathers up the empty sheaves
    When all the golden grain is done.

DOWN THE MISSISSIPPI AT NIGHT.

Sowing the waves with a fiery rain,
   Leaving behind us a lane of light,
   Weaving a web in the woof of night,
Cleaving a continent's wealth in twain.

Lighting the world with a way of flame,
   Writing, even as the lightnings write
   High over the awful arched forehead of night,
Jehovah's dread and unutterable name.

LA EXPOSICION.

NEW ORLEANS.

The banners!   The bells!   The red banners!
   The rainbows of banners!   The chimes!
The music of stars!   The sweet manners
   Of peace in old pastoral times!

The coming of nations!   Kings bringing
   Rich gifts to Republics!   The trees
Of paradise, and birds singing
   By the side of De Soto's swift seas!

A NUBIAN FACE ON THE NILE.

One night we touched the lily shore,
And then passed on, in night indeed,
Against the far white waterfall.
I saw no more, shall know no more
Of her for aye. And you who read
This broken bit of dream will smile,
Half vexed that I saw aught at all.
The waves struck strophes on the shore
And all the sad song of the oar
That long, long night against the Nile,
Was: Nevermore and nevermore
This side that shadowy shore that lies
Below the leafy Paradise.

THE WORLD IS A BETTER WORLD.

Aye, the world is a better world to-day!
   And a great good mother this earth of ours;
Her white to-morrows are a white stairway
   To lead us up to the star-lit flowers—
The spiral to-morrows that one by one
We climb and we climb in the face of the sun.

Aye, the world is a braver world to-day!
   For many a hero will bear with wrong—
Will laugh at wrong and will turn away;
   Will whistle it down the wind with a song—
Will slay the wrong with his splendid scorn!
The bravest hero that ever was born!

LINCOLN PARK.

   UNWALLED it lies, and open as the sun
When God swings wide the dark doors of the East.
   Oh, keep this one spot, still keep this one,
Where tramp or banker, layman or high priest,
May equal meet before the face of God.
Yea, equals stand upon that common sod
Where they shall one day equals be
Beneath, for aye, and all eternity.

MONTGOMERY AT QUEBEC.

Sword in hand he was slain;
   The snow his winding;
   The grinding ice at his feet—
The river moaning in pain.

Pity and peace at last;
   Flowers for him to-day
   Above on the battlements gray--
And the river rolling past.

MAGNOLIA BLOSSOMS.

The broad magnolia's blooms are white;
   Her blooms are large, as if the moon
Had lost her way some lazy night,
   And lodged here till the afternoon.

Oh, vast white blossoms breathing love!
   White bosom of my lady dead,
   In your white heaven overhead
I look, and learn to look above.

MANITOBA.

O NEIGHBORS, neighbors, rouse you! Quick!
　My hearth is empty and forlorn,
My heart is empty, faint and sick,
　For John came dragging home at morn
Two frozen limbs, and oh! and oh!
My boy left buried in the snow!

Nay, blame not John. The day was wild
　With driving snow that drowned his face.
The hidden sleigh now holds my child,
　The horse stands frozen in his place.
Come, neighbors, quick! Be not so slow!
My boy lies buried in the snow.

The snow is frozen; follow me!
　Like ice this gleaming sea of snow!
And far across the frozen sea
　The mound where he is lying low.
Oh, like to gold his hair; his eyes
Were borrowed bits of yonder skies.

I clad my boy as best I had.
　The sleigh sped ringing toward the mill.
My boy ! my poor, lost farmer lad !
　Oh, that I had you with me still !
Why, I would give these snowy lands
To knit two mittens for his hands !

But, neighbors, neighbors, here !　Behold
　This mound of snow, this broken place !
A sweet face in a sheen of gold !
　Oh ! two blue eyes laughing in my face !
My boy, my boy, safe, sound and well,
Breaks like a chicken from his shell !

THE NEW PRESIDENT.

Granite and marble and granite,
  Corridor, column and dome!
A capitol huge as a planet
  And massive as marble-built Rome.

Stair steps of granite to glory!
  Go up with thy face to the sun;
They are stained with the footsteps and story
  Of giants and battles well won.

Stop— stand on this stairway of granite,
  Lo! Arlington, storied and still,
With a lullaby hush. But the land it
  Springs fresh as that sun-fronted hill.

Beneath us stout-hearted Potomac
  In majesty moves to the sea—
Beneath us a sea of proud people
  Moves on, undivided as he.

Yea, strife it is over and ended
    For all the days under the sun ;
The banners unite and are blended
    As moonlight and sunlight in one.

Lo ! banners and banners and banners,
    Broad star-balanced banners of blue—
If a single star fell from fair heaven,
    Why, what would befall us, think you ?

Lo ! westward and northward and southward
    The captains come home from the wars—
Now the world shall endure if we only
    Keep perfect this system of stars.

THE RIVER OF REST.

A BEAUTIFUL stream is the River of Rest;
   The still, wide waters sweep clear and cold,
A tall mast crosses a star in the west,
   A white sail gleams in the west world's gold:
It leans to the shore of the River of Rest—
The lily-lined shore of the River of Rest.

The boatman rises, he reaches a hand,
   He knows you well, he will steer you true,
And far, so far, from all ills upon land,
   From hates, from fates that pursue and pursue;
Far over the lily-lined River of Rest—
Dear mystical, magical River of Rest.

A storied, sweet stream is this River of Rest;
   The souls of all time keep its ultimate shore;
And journey you east or journey you west,
   Unwilling, or willing, sure footed or sore,
You surely will come to this River of Rest—
This beautiful, beautiful River of Rest.

"LA NOTTE."

Is it night? And sits at night your pillow?
    Sits darkness about you like death?
Rolls darkness above like a billow,
    As drowning men catch in their breath?

Is it night, and deep night of dark errors,
    Of crosses, of pitfalls and bars?
Then lift up your face from your terrors,
    For heaven alone holds the stars!

Lo! shaggy-beard shepherds, the fastness—
    Lorn, desolate Syrian sod;
The darkness, the midnight, the vastness—
    That vast, solemn night bore a God!

That night brought us God! and the Savior
    Lay down in a manger to rest;
A sweet cherub Babe in behavior,
    So that all Baby-world might be blest.

CALIFORNIA'S CHRISTMAS.

The stars are large as lilies!   Morn
   Seems some illumined story—
The story of our Savior born,
   Told from yon turrets hoary—
The full moon smiling tips a horn
   And hies to bed in glory!

My sunclad city walks in light
   And lasting summer weather;
Red roses bloom on bosoms white
   And rosy cheeks together.
If you should smite one cheek, still smite
   For she will turn the other.

The thronged warm street tides to and fro
   And Love, roseclad, discloses.
The only snowstorm we shall know
   Is this white storm of roses—
It seems like Maytime, mating so,
   And—Nature counting noses.

CALIFORNIA'S CHRISTMAS.

Soft sea winds sleep on yonder tide ;
   You hear some boatmen rowing.
Their sisters' hands trail o'er the side ;
   They toy with warm waves flowing ;
Their laps are laden deep and wide
   From rose-trees green and growing.

Such roses white ! such roses red !
   Such roses richly yellow !
The air is like a perfume fed
   From autumn fruits full mellow—
But see ! a brother bends his head,
   An oar forgets its fellow !

Give me to live in land like this,
   Nor let me wander further ;
Some sister in some boat of bliss
   And I her only brother—
Sweet paradise on earth it is ;
   I would not seek another.

THOSE PERILOUS SPANISH EYES

    Some fragrant trees,
    Some flower-sown seas
Where boats go up and down,
    And a sense of rest
    To the tired breast
In that beauteous Aztec town.

But the terrible thing in that Aztec town
   That will blow men's rest to the stormiest skies,
Or whether they journey or they lie down—
   Those perilous Spanish eyes!

    Snow walls without,
    Drawn sharp about
To prop the sapphire skies!
    Two huge gate-posts,
    Snow-white like ghosts—
Gate-posts to this paradise!

But, oh! turn back from the high-walled town!
   There is trouble enough in this world, I surmise,
Without men riding in regiments down—
   Oh, those perilous Spanish eyes!

NEWPORT NEWS.

The huge sea monster, the "Merrimac;"
The mad sea monster, the "Monitor;"
You may sweep the sea, peer forward and back,
But never a sign or a sound of war.
   A vulture or two in the heavens blue;
      A sweet town building, a boatman's call;
   The far sea-song of a pleasure crew;
      The sound of hammers. And that is all.

And where are the monsters that tore this main?
And where are the monsters that shook this shore?
The sea grew mad! And the shore shot flame!
The mad sea monsters they are no more.
   The palm, and the pine, and the sea-sands brown;
      The far sea-songs of the pleasure crews;
   The air like balm in this building town—
      And that is the picture of Newport News..

THE TRUE POET.

O, HEARD ye the eloquent song of God's silence?
    The vines are His lines; and the emerald sod,
The page of His book, and the green-girdled islands
    Are rocked to their rest in the cradle of God.

God's poet is silence! His song is unspoken
    And yet so profound, and so loud, and so far,
That it thrills you and fills you in measures unbroken—
    The unceasing song of the first morning star.

The shallow seas moan! As a child they have muttered,
    And mourned, and lamented, and wept at their will;
The poems of God are too good to be uttered—
    The dreadful deep seas, they are loudest when still.

COMING.

My own and my only Love some night
    Shall keep her tryst, shall come from the South,
And oh, her robe of magnolia white!
    And oh, and oh, the breath of her mouth!

And oh, her grace in the grasses sweet!
    And oh, her love in the leaves new born!
And oh, and oh, her lily-white feet
    Set daintily down in the dew-wet morn!

The drowsy cattle at night shall kneel
    And give God thanks, and shall dream and rest;
The stars slip down and a golden seal
    Be set on the meadows my Love has blest.

Come back, my Love, come sudden, come soon.
    The world lies waiting as the cold dead lie;
The frightened winds wail and the crisp-curled moon
    Rides, wrapped in clouds, up the cold gray sky.

Oh, Summer, my Love, my first, last Love!
  I sit all day by Potomac here,
Waiting and waiting the voice of the dove—
  Waiting my darling, my own, my dear.

BY THE BALBOA SEAS.

The golden fleece is at our feet,
   Our hills are girt in sheen of gold;
Our golden flower-fields are sweet
   With honey hives. A thousand-fold
More fair our fruits on laden stem
Than Jordan's tow'rd Jerusalem.

Beneath our ancient cloud-clad trees
   The ages pass in silence by.
Gold apples of Hesperides
   Hang at our God-land gates for aye.
Our golden shores have golden keys
Where sound and sing the Balboa seas.

"TO DIE FOR THE COUNTRY."

"Peace hath her victories no less renowned than war."

To die for the country! when dying comes
   It is not for the flag, it is not for the land,
   It is not for the glory, the battle grand—
For all the cannon and the roll of drums!

The prayer is not for the flag in the fight,
   But ever for home, for babe and for wife;
   For life and the loved ones—life, sweet life—
And that is the prayer in the battle's night!

I tell you, to see the man at your side
   Sink down as you hear that sickening thud—
   To look in his face, to see the blood
Slow oozing from lips that have lost their pride!

I tell you to see his brimming eyes swim!
   I tell you, to see him clutch to the mold
   And grasp at the grass, as if to hold
The earth from passing away from him!

"TO DIE FOR THE COUNTRY."

Oh, ye who have witnessed the dying in heaps,
    The Northerner heaped with the Southerner,
Just as the hastening reaper reaps
    Blossoms and corn and cockle burr!

Answer and say if ever a breath
    Was heard of delight to die for the land?
    Nay, only the reach of a helpless hand
To hold each back from the banks of death.

Nothing at all, in that last despair,
    Of the one last shot in the desperate strife;
But only a prayer, a low last prayer
    For her at the last, and for life, sweet life!

Nothing at all of a sword from the sheath
    For the one last blow from the field afar,
But only a prayer; then grinding of teeth,
    And a curse upon those who compelled the war.

For, oh! it is hard for the man to go,
    So many are waiting him far away;
He can hear his kindly-eyed cattle low;
    He can see his wife and her babes at play.

So he who says it is sweet to die
    For country has never yet felt or seen
    The shock of battle or the sheaves between,
And tells you a pitiful Pagan's lie.

OUR HEROES OF TO-DAY.

I.

With high face held to her ultimate star,
   With swift feet set to her mountains of gold,
This new-built world, where the wonders are,
   She has built new ways from the ways of old.

II.

Her builders of worlds are workers with hands;
   Her true world-builders are builders of these,
The engines, the plows; writing poems in sands
   Of gold in our golden Hesperides.

III.

I reckon these builders as gods among men:
   I count them creators, creators who knew
The thrill of dominion, of conquest, as when
   God set His stars spinning their spaces of blue.

IV.

A song for these soldiers of peace; and again
   A song for the marvels these men have wrought;
Our gleamy snows, and their bredes of grain
   If unrolled as a scroll could record them not.

V.

A song for the groove, and a song for the wheel,
    And a roaring song for the rumbling car;
But away with the pomp of the soldier's steel,
    And away forever with the trade of war.

VI.

The hero of time is the hero of thought;
    The hero who lives is the hero of peace;
And braver his battles than ever were fought,
    From Shiloh back to the battles of Greece.

VII.

The hero of heroes is the engineer;
    The hero of height and of gnome-built deep,
Whose only fear is the brave man's fear
    That someone waiting at home might weep.

VIII.

The hero we love in this land to-day
    Is the hero who lightens some fellow-man's load—
Who makes of the mountain some pleasant highway;
    Who makes of the desert some blossom-sown road.

IX.

The Stanfords, the Sutros and the Hallidays,
    And an hundred more with their names untold—
They are kinglier far in their uncrowned ways
    Than ever were kings with their crowns of gold.

X.

Then hurrah! for the land of the golden downs,
    For the fruitful land of the silver horn;
Her heroes have built her a thousand towns,
    But never destroyed her one blade of corn.

THE LOST BOY REGIMENTS.

It was terror to left, it was terror to right,
   The gunboats came cleaving their way through the land--
Came shouting by day and shelling by night,
   With cities in ashes on either hand—
The great iron monsters incessantly
Shelling and shelling their way to the sea !

And only veterans, gray that day—
   Gray in the glory of God's uniform,
And marshaled and ready to march away
   To that great roll-call that shall ride the storm,
Only women and these old men gray,
And schoolboys fighting in mimic fray.

For emptied of men was the land to the main;
   They had gone to the wars, they were far away.
But mothers cried out, as in travail pain,
   And boys grew to men on that battle day !
And boys grew to men in their brave intents—
Came shouting and rushing in regiments;

Came manning the dykes up the cypress wood,
 The brave boy-regiments born in a day,
And under the dykes in battle line stood,
 With cannon and muskets in battle array.
Ay, breathless and eager in brave defense
Stood waiting the stern boy-regiments.

Then smoke burst forth from the great gunboats!
 And iron and steel came tearing into
The wood-built dykes from the iron throats
 Till the dykes were broken, and booming through
The riddled old walls and the widening rents
The waves rolled over the regiments!

Their muskets lay mute in their watery graves,
 Their cannon had never one word to say;
Their red mouths washed by the rushing waves
 And lost in the marshes were the men in gray.
The great gunboats sailed on as before,
Shelling and shelling the flame-lit shore!

Their muskets, their cannon, have nothing to say,
 They are rusting to-day by the great swamp trees,
Gray cypress-trees kneeling on rugged old knees,
 As gray monks kneel by their dead to pray.
And fireflies volley and volley in vain
To call the boy-regiments back again.

BY THE LOWER MISSISSIPPI.

The king of rivers has a dolorous shore,
    A dreamful dominion of cypress-trees,
A gray bird rising forever more,
    And drifting away toward the Mexican seas—
A lone bird seeking for some lost mate,
So dolorous, lorn and desolate.

The shores are gray as the sands are gray;
    And gray are the trees in their cloaks of moss;—
That gray bird rising and drifting away,
    Slow dragging its weary long legs across—
So weary, just over the gray wood's brink;
It wearies one, body and soul, to think.

These vast gray levels of cypress wood,
    The gray soldiers' graves; and so, God's will—
These cypress-trees' roots are still running blood:
    The smoke of battle in their mosses still—
That gray bird wearily drifting away
Was startled some long-since battle day.

HER PICTURE.

I SEE her now—the fairest thing
That ever mocked man's picturing,
I picture her as one who drew
Aside life's curtain and looked through
The mists of all life's mystery
As from a wood to open sea.

I picture her as one who knew
How rare is truth to be untrue—
As one who knew the awful sign
Of death, of life, of the divine
Sweet pity of all loves, all hates,
Beneath the iron-footed fates.

I picture her as seeking peace,
   And olive leaves and vine-set land;
   While strife stood by on either hand,
And wrung her tears like rosaries.
I picture her in passing rhyme
   As of, yet not a part of, these—
A woman born above her time.

The soft, wide eyes of wonderment
   That trusting looked you through and through;
The sweet, arched mouth, a bow new bent,
   That sent love's arrow swift and true.

That sweet, arched mouth! The Orient
   Hath not such pearls in all her stores,
   Nor all her storied, spice-set shores
Have fragrance such as it hath spent.

DROWNED.

A FIG for her story of shame and of pride!
    She strayed in the night and her feet fell astray;
    The great Mississippi was glad that day,
And that is the reason the poor girl died;
    The great Mississippi was glad, I say,
And splendid with strength in his fierce full pride—
And that is the reason the poor girl died.

And that was the reason, from first to last;
    Down under the dark, still cypresses there
The Father of Waters he held her fast.
    He kissed her face, he fondled her hair,
No more, no more an unloved outcast,
    He clasped her close to his great, strong breast,
    Brave lover that loved her last and best.

Around and around in her watery world,
    Down under the boughs where the bank hung steep,
And cypress-trees kneeled all gnarly and curled,
    Where woods were dark as the waters were deep,

Where strong, swift waters were swept and swirled,
  Where the whirlpool sobbed and sucked in its breath,
  As some great monster that is choking to death:

Where sweeping and swirling around and around
  That whirlpool eddied so dark and so deep
That even a populous world might have drowned,
  So surging, so vast, and so swift its sweep—
  She rode on the wave. And the trees that weep,
The solemn gray cypresses leaning o'er ;
The roots ran blood as they leaned from the shore !

She surely was drowned ! But she should have been
      still ;
  She should have been dead as the dead under
      ground ;
She should have been still as the dead on the hill !
  But ever and ever she eddied around,
  And so nearer and nearer she drew me there
  Till her eyes met mine in their cold dead stare.

Then she looked, and she looked as to look me through ;
  And she came so close to my feet on the shore.
  And her large eyes, larger than ever before,
They never grew weary as dead men's do.
  And her hair ! as long as the moss that swept
  From the cypress-trees as they leaned and wept.

Then the moon rose up, and she came to see,
  Her long white fingers slow pointing there;
Why, shoulder to shoulder the moon with me
  On the bank that night, with her shoulders bare,
  Slow pointing and pointing that white face out,
  As it swirled and it swirled, and it swirled about.

There ever and ever, around and around,
  Those great sad eyes that refused to sleep!
  Reproachful sad eyes that had ceased to weep!
And the great whirlpool with its gurgling sound!
  The reproachful dead that was not yet dead!
  The long strong hair from that shapely head!

Her hair was so long! so marvelous long,
  As she rode and she rode on that whirlpool's breast;
And she rode so swift, and she rode so strong,
Never to rest as the dead should rest.
  Oh, tell me true, could her hair in the wave
  Have grown, as grow dead men's in the grave?

For, hist! I have heard that a virgin's hair
  Will grow in the grave of a virgin true,
Will grow and grow in the coffin there,
Till head and foot it is filled with hair
  All silken and soft—but what say you?
  Yea, tell me truly can this be true?

For oh, her hair was so strangely long
　　That it bound her about like a veil of night,
　　With only her pitiful face in sight !
As she rode so swift, and she rode so strong,
　　That it wrapped her about, as a shroud had done,
　　A shroud, a coffin, and a veil in one.

And oh, that ride on the whirling tide !
　　That whirling and whirling it is in my head,
　　For the eyes of my dead they are not yet dead,
Though surely the lady had long since died.
　　Then the mourning wood by the watery grave ;
　　The moon's white face to the face in the wave.

That moon I shall hate ! For she left her place
Unasked up in heaven to show me that face.
　　I shall hate forever the sounding tide ;
For oh, that swirling it is in my head
As it swept and it swirled with my dead not dead,
　　And it gasped and it sobbed as a God that died.

AFTER THE BATTLE.

Sing banners and cannon and roll of drum!
   The shouting of men and the marshaling!
Lo! cannon to cannon and earth struck dumb!
   Oh, battle, in song, is a glorious thing!

Oh, glorious day, riding down to the fight!
   Oh, glorious battle in story and song!
Oh, godlike man to die for the right!
   Oh, manlike God to revenge the wrong!

Yea, riding to battle, on battle day—
   Why, a soldier is something more than a king!
But after the battle! The riding away!
   Ah, the riding away is another thing!

MY COUNTRY.

My country, what is it ? A place that is dear
   From holy traditions of dear baby land,
From faces long vanished, from dust we revere,
   From friendships of boyhood that grew hand in hand
And merged into manhood as year knit to year.

My country, where is it ? The place where I knew
   A dear mother's face, where God sat me down
At the first, where I gathered my strength, where I
      grew
   To believe the fair limits that girded me round
The down-falling curtains of heaven's own blue.

My country, where is it ? The place where the soul
   Takes color, takes form and expression and size ;
   The spot where the star-studded scroll of the skies
Proclaims my protection, that volumes the whole
   Of love, of existence, of all that men prize.

My country, where is it ? The icy North Pole,
  Or any north land, or land anywhere,
  May be sacred to others, be fond or be fair :
But my own natal skies are a legible scroll
  With the dear name of MOTHER indelibly there.

AFTER THE WAR.

Yes, bread! I want bread! You heard what I said,
  Yet you stand and you stare,
As if never before came a tramp to your door
  With such insolent air.

Would I work? Never learned.—*My* home it was
    burned;
  And I haven't yet found
Any heart to plow lands and build homes for red
    hands
  That burned mine to the ground.

No bread! you have said?—Then my curse on your
    head!
  And, what shall sting worse,
On that wife at your side, on those babes in their
    pride,
  Fall my seven-fold curse!—

Good bye! I must l'arn to creep into your barn;
   Suck your eggs; hide away;
Sneak around like a hound—light a match in your
      hay—
   Limp away through the gray!

Yes, I limp—curse these stones! And then my old
      bones—
   They were riddled with ball
Down at Shiloh. What, you? You war wounded
      thar, too?
   Well, you beat us—that's all.

Yet even *my* heart with a stout pride will start
   As I tramp. For, you see,
No matter which won, it was gallantly done,
   And a glorious American victory.

What, kind words and bread? God's smiles on your
      head!
   On your wife on your babes!—and please, sir, I
      pray
You'll pardon me, sir; but that fight trenched me
      here,
   Deep—deeper than sword-cut that day.

Nay. I'll go. Sir, adieu! *Tu Tityre* * * * You
  Have Augustus for friend —
I—Yes, read and speak both Latin and Greek,
  And talk slang without end.

Hey? Oxford. But, then, when the wild cry for men
  Rang out through the gathering night
As a mother who cries for her first born that dies,
  We two hurried home for the fight.

How noble my brother, how brave—and—but there—
  This tramping about somehow hurts my eyes.
At Shiloh! We stood 'neath the hill by the wood—
  It's a graveyard to-day, I surmise.

Yes we stood to the last! And when the strife
      passed
  I sank down in blood at his side.
On his brow, on his breast—what need tell the rest?—
  I but knew that my brother had died.

What! wounds on *your* breast? *Your* brow tells the
      rest?
  You fought at my side and *you* fell?
You the brave boy that stood at my side in that wood.
  On that blazing red border of hell?

My brother! My own! Never king on his throne
  Knew a joy like this brought to me.
God bless you, my life; bless your brave Northern
    wife,
  And your beautiful babes, two and three.

BY THE PACIFIC OCEAN.

Here room and kingly silence keep
   Companionship in state austere,
   The dignity of death is here,
The large, lone vastness of the deep.
   Here toil has pitched his camp to rest,
   The west is banked against the west.

Above yon gleaming skies of gold
   One lone imperial peak is seen;
   While gathered at his feet in green
Ten thousand foresters are told.
   And all so still! so still the air
   That duty drops the web of care.

Beneath the sunset's golden sheaves
   The awful deep walks with the deep,
   Where silent sea-doves slip and sweep,
And commerce keeps her loom and weaves.
   The dead red men refuse to rest;
   Their ghosts illume my lurid West.

BY THE GREAT RIVER.

Oh, lion of the ample earth,
    What sword can cleave thy sinews through?
    The South forever cradles you;
And yet the great North gives you birth.

Go find an arm so strong, so sure,
    Go forge a sword so keen, so true,
    That it can thrust thy bosom through;
Then may this Union not endure!

In orange lands I lean to-day
    Against thy warm tremendous mouth,
    Oh, tawny lion of the South,
To hear what story you shall say.

What story of the stormy North,
    Of frost-bound homes, of babes at play—
    What tale of twenty States the day
You left your lair and leapt forth:

The day you tore the mountain's breast
    And in the icy North uprose,
    And shook your sides of rains and snows,
And rushed against the South to rest :

Oh, tawny river, what of they,
    The far North folk ? The maiden sweet—
    The ardent lover at her feet—
What story of thy States to-day !

    *   *   *   *   *   *

The river kissed my garment's hem,
    And whispered as it swept away :
    "God's story in all States to-day
Is of a babe of Bethlehem."

GRANT AT SHILOH.

The blue and the gray! Their work was well done!
   They lay as to listen to the waters flow.
Some lay with their faces upturned to the sun,
   As seeking to know what the gods might know.
Their work was well done, each soldier was true.
But what is the question that comes to you?

For all that men do, for all that men dare,
   That river still runs with its stateliest flow.
The sun and the moon I scarcely think care
   A fig for the fallen, of friend or of foe.
But the moss-mantled cypress, the old soldiers say,
Still mantles in smoke of that battle day!

These men in the dust! These pitiful dead!
   The gray and the blue, the blue and the gray,
The headless trunk and the trunkless head;
   The image of God in the gory clay!
And who was the bravest? Say, can you tell
If Death throws dice with a loaded shell?

TWILIGHT ON OAKLAND HEIGHTS.

The brave young city by the Balboa seas
  Lies compassed about by the hosts of night—
Lies humming, low, like a hive of bees;
  And the day lies dead. And its spirit's flight
Is far to the west; while the golden bars
That bound it are broken to a dust of stars.

Come under my oaks, oh, drowsy dusk!
  The wolf and the dog; dear incense hour
When Mother Earth hath a smell of musk,
  And things of the spirit assert their power—
When candles are set to burn in the west—
Set head and foot to the day at rest.

THE BIRTH OF CALIFORNIA'S ARBOR DAY.

"The address was by Hon. John P. Irish. He believed tree-planting originated in Nebraska, twenty-six years ago, where the wide plains had been made to yield rich harvests through this custom, the arable land steadily moving westward at the rate of three miles every year, as the trees were planted. In that State, and in others that had followed Nebraska's example, Arbor Day was a legal holiday, and he hoped to see the occasion entrenched as a legal holiday in the laws of this State. He was glad that this movement was due to the inspiration of Joaquin Miller, because he is to live in the world's immortal literature as the poet of the Sierras, along whose slopes man's hand is wasting God's prodigal gifts. It was eminently appropriate that to this poet's inspiration these mountains should be reclothed with their emerald robes and made majestic in their forests and groves. "Every tree is a tree of life, for it contains that which sustains life and gives to us a knowledge that leads us to a higher contemplation of the works of God. To-day we plant the tree of life and the tree of knowledge."

Governor Perkins and General Howard spoke of the poet's "Crusade Cross of Arbor Day."

ARBOR DAY.

Against our golden orient dawns
   We lift a living light to-day,
That shall outshine the splendid bronze
   That lords and lights that lesser Bay.

Sweet Paradise was sown with trees,
   Thy very name, lorn Nazareth,
Means woods, means sense of birds and bees,
   And song of leaves with lisping breath.

God gave us Mother Earth, full blest
   With robes of green in healthful fold ;
We tore the green robes from her breast !
   We sold our mother's robes for gold !

We sold her garments fair, and she
   Lies shamed and naked at our feet !
In penitence we plant a tree ;
   We plant the cross and count it meet.

Lo, here, where Balboa's waters toss,
   Here in this glorious Spanish bay,
We plant the cross, the Christian cross,
   The Crusade Cross of Arbor Day.

PETER COOPER.

DIED 1883.

Give honor and love forevermore
    To this great man gone to rest;
Peace on the dim Plutonian shore,
    Rest in the land of the blest.

I reckon him greater than any man
    That ever drew sword in war;
I reckon him nobler than king or khan,
    Braver and better by far.

And wisest he in this whole wide land
    Of hoarding till bent and gray;
For all you can hold in your cold dead hand
    Is what you have given away.

So, whether to wander the stars or to rest
    Forever hushed and dumb,
He gave with a zest and he gave his best—
    Give him the best to come.

A. T. STEWART.

[The preceding lines are already in one of my books, but I put them here for the purpose of antithesis. I have forgotten when this last-named man died. I doubt if anybody cares to know. I doubt if anybody even knows where he is buried.

Of course I shall be abused for doing what I do. But I have my duties. And I shall stand stoutly up against the face of the world in its foolish deification of gold when I think it best.]

    The gold that with the sunlight lies
        In bursting heaps at dawn,
    The silver spilling from the skies
        At night to walk upon,
    The diamonds gleaming with the dew
    He never saw, he never knew.

    He got some gold, dug from the mud,
        Some silver, crushed from stones.
    The gold was red with dead men's blood,
        The silver black with groans.
    And when he died he moaned aloud
    "There'll be no pocket in my shroud !"

THE LARGER COLLEGE.

ON LAYING THE COLLEGE CORNER-STONE.

Where San Diego seas are warm,
    Where winter winds from warm Cathay
Sing sibilant, where blossoms swarm
    With Hybla's bees, we come to lay
This tribute of the truest, best,
    The warmest daughter of the West.

Here Progress plants her corner-stone
    Against this warm, still, Cortez wave.
In ashes of the Aztec's throne,
    In tummals of the Toltec's grave,
We plant this stone, and from the sod
    Pick painted fragments of his god.

Here Progress lifts her torch to teach
    God's pathway through the pass of care;
Her altar-stone Balboa's Beach,
    Her incense warm, sweet, perfumed air;
Such incense! where white strophes reach
    And lap and lave Balboa's Beach!

We plant this stone as some small seed
   Is sown at springtime, warm with earth;
We sow this seed as some good deed
   Is sown, to grow until its worth
Shall grow, through rugged steeps of time,
To touch the God-built stars sublime.

We lift this lighthouse by the sea,
   The westmost sea, the westmost shore,
To guide man's ship of destiny
   When Scylla and Charybdis roar;
To teach him strength, to proudly teach
God's grandeur, where His white palms reach:

To teach not Sybil books alone;
   Man's books are but a climbing stair,
Lain step by step, like stairs of stone;
   The stairway here, the temple there—
Man's lampad honor, and his trust,
The God who called him from the dust.

Man's books are but man's alphabet,
   Beyond and on his lessons lie—
The lessons of the violet,
   The large gold letters of the sky;
The love of beauty, blossomed soil,
The large content, the tranquil toil:

The toil that nature ever taught,
    The patient toil, the constant stir,
The toil of seas where shores are wrought,
    The toil of Christ, the carpenter;
The toil of God incessantly
By palm-set land or frozen sea.

Behold this sea, that sapphire sky!
    Where nature does so much for man,
Shall man not set his standard high,
    And hold some higher, holier plan?
Some loftier plan than ever planned
By outworn book of outworn land?

Where God has done so much for man,
    Shall man for God do aught at all?
The soul that feeds on books alone—
    I count that soul exceeding small
That lives alone by book and creed,—
A soul that has not learned to read.

These broad banana leaves shall teach
    The larger lesson. Read who will
Their wider page, their broader reach
    Of thought, of creed, profounder skill,
The red-lipped laughter of their bloom,—
A torch that leads from out our tomb!

The light is on us, and such light!
   Such perfumed warmth of winter sea!
Such musky smell of maiden night!
   Such bridal bough and orange-tree!
Such wondrous stars! Yon lily moon
Seems like some long-lost afternoon!

More perfect than a string of pearls
   We hold the full days of the year;
The days troop by like flower girls,
   And all the days are ours here.
Here youth must learn; here age may live
Full tide each day the year can give.

No frosted wall, no frozen hasp,
   Shuts Nature's book from us to-day;
Her palm-leaves lift too high to clasp;
   Her college walls the milky way.
The light is with us! Read and lead!
The larger book, the loftier deed!

THE POEM BY THE POTOMAC.

Two or three hundred steps to the right and up a general incline and you stand on the broad, high porch of Mount Vernon.

A great river creeps close underneath one hundred feet or two below. You might suppose you could throw a stone, standing on the porch, into the Potomac as seen through the trees, that hug the hillside and the water's bank below. All is quiet, so quiet. Now and then a barnyard fowl, back in the rear, strained his glossy neck and called out loud and clear in the eternal Sabbath here; a fine shaggy dog wallowed and romped about the grassy dooryard, while far out over the vast river some black, wide-winged birds kept circling round and round. I went back and around into the barnyard to inquire what kind of birds they were. I met a very respectful but very stammery negro here. He took his cap in his hand, and twisting it all about and opening his mouth many times, he finally said:

"Do-do-dose burds was created by de Lord to p-p-pu-purify de yearth."

"But what do you call them, uncle?"

"Tur-tur-tur," and he twisted his cap, backed out, came forward, winked his eyes, but could not go on.

"Do you mean turkey buzzards?"

"Ya-ya-yas, sah, do-do-dose burds eats up de carrion ob de yearth, sah."

Down yonder is the tomb, the family vault. Back in the rear of the two marble coffins about thirty of the Washington family lie. The vault is locked up and closed forever. The key has been thrown into the trusty old Potomac to lie there until the last trump shall open all tombs.

Let no one hereafter complain of having to live in a garret alone and without a fire. For here, with all this spacious and noble house to select from, the widow of Washington chose a garret looking to the south and out upon his tomb. This is the old tomb where he was first laid to rest and where the fallen oak leaves are crowding in heaps now and almost filling up the low, dark doorway.

This garret has but one window, a small and narrow dormer window, and is otherwise quite dark. A bottom corner of the door is cut away so that her cat might come and go at will. And this is the saddest, tenderest sight at Mount Vernon. It seemed to me that I could see this noble lady sitting here, looking out upon the tomb of her mighty dead, the great river sweeping fast beyond, her heart full of the memory of a mighty Nation's birth, waiting, waiting, waiting.

The thing, however, of the most singular interest here is a key of the Bastile, presented by Thomas Paine to Lafayette, who brought it to America and presented it to Washington. It hangs here in a glass case, massive and monstrous. It is a hideous, horrible thing and has, perhaps, more blood and misery on it than any other piece of iron or steel that ever was seen.

THE POEM BY THE POTOMAC.

PAINE! The Prison of France! Lafayette!
   The Bastile key to our Washington,
Whose feet on the neck of tyrants set
   Shattered their prisons every one.

The key hangs here on his white walls high,
That all shall see, that none shall forget
What tyrants have been, what they may be yet;
  And the Potomac rolling by.

On Washington's walls let it rust and rust,
  And tell its story of blood and of tears,
That Time still holds to the Poet's trust,
  To people his pages for years and years.
  The monstrous shape on the white walls high,
Like a thief in chains let it rot and rust—
Its kings and adorers crowned in dust:
  And the Potomac rolling by.

A DEAD CARPENTER.

What shall be said of this soldier now dead?
　　This builder, this brother, now resting forever?
What shall be said of this soldier who bled
　　Through thirty-three years of silent endeavor?

Why, name him thy hero! Yea, write his name down
　　As something far nobler, as braver by far
Than purple-robed Cæsar of battle-torn town
　　When bringing home glittering trophies of war.

Oh, dark somber pines of my starlit Sierras,
　　Be silent of song, for the master is mute!
The Carpenter, master, is dead and lo! there is
　　Silence of song upon nature's draped lute!

Brother! Oh, manly dead brother of mine!
　　My brother by toil 'mid the toiling and lowly,
My brother by sign of this hard hand, by sign
　　Of toil, and hard toil, that the Christ has made holy;

Yea, brother of all the brave millions that toil!
　Brave brother in patience and silent endeavor,
Rest, as the harvester rich from his soil,
　Rest you, and rest you for ever and ever.

BACK TO THE GOLDEN GATE

Yea, I have tracked the hemispheres,
    Have touched on fairest land that lies
    This side the gates of Paradise;
Have ranged the universe for years;
    Have read the book of love right on,
From title leaf to colophon.

THE FORTUNATE ISLES.

You sail and you seek for the Fortunate Isles,
   The old Greek Isles of the yellow-birds' song?
Then steer straight on through the watery miles,
   Straight on, straight on and you can't go wrong.
Nay not to the left, nay not to the right,
But on, straight on, and the Isles are in sight,
The Fortunate Isles where the yellow-birds sing
And life lies girt with a golden ring.

These Fortunate Isles they are not so far,
   They lie within reach of the lowliest door;
You can see them gleam by the twilight star;
   You can hear them sing by the moon's white shore—
Nay, never look back! Those leveled grave-stones
They were landing steps; they were steps unto thrones
Of glory for souls that have sailed before,
And have set white feet on the fortunate shore.

And what are the names of the Fortunate Isles?
   Why, Duty and Love and a large content.
Lo! these are the Isles of the watery miles,
   That God let down from the firmament.

Lo! Duty, and Love, and a true man's trust;
Your forehead to God though your feet in the dust;
Lo! Duty, and Love, and a sweet babe's smiles,
And these, O friend, are the Fortunate Isles.

THE SIZE OF SOULS.

Didst never think how souls have size,
And weight, and measure, in God's eyes
So different from weight and span
And measure given them by man?

SIERRA.

With vast foundations seamed and knit,
    And wrought and bound by golden bars,
Sierra's peaks serenely sit
    And challenge heaven's sentry-stars.

QUEBEC.

She gleams above a granite throne;
Her gray walls gird her ample zone;
She queens the North, supreme—alone!

DEAD IN THE LONG, STRONG GRASS.

Born to the saddle and bred by a chain of events to ride with the wind until I met the stolid riders of England, I can now see how it was that Anthony Trollope, Lord Houghton and others of the saddle and "meet" gave me ready place in their midst. Not that the English were less daring; but they were less fortunate; may, I say less experienced. I recall the fact that I once found Lord Houghton's brother, Lord Crewe, and his son also, under the hands of the surgeon in York; one with a broken thigh, and the other with a few broken ribs. But in all our hard riding I never had a scratch.

One morning Trollope hinted that my immunity was due to my big Spanish saddle, which I had brought from Mexico City. I threw my saddle on the grass and rode without so much as a blanket. And I rode neck to neck; and then left them all behind and nearly everyone unhorsed.

Prince Napoleon was of the party that morning; and as the gentlemen pulled themselves together on the return he kept by my side, and finally proposed a tour through Notts and Sherwood Forest on horseback. And so it fell out that we rode together much.

But he had already been persistently trained in the slow military methods; and it was in vain that I tried to teach him to cling to his horse and climb into the saddle as he ran, after the fashion of Indians and vaqueros. He admired it greatly, but seemed to think it unbecoming a soldier.

It was at the Literary Fund dinner, where Stanley and Prince Napoleon stood together when they made their speeches, that I saw this brave and brilliant young man for the last time. He was about to set out for Africa with the English troops to take part in the Zulu war.

He seemed very serious. When about to separate he took my hand, and, looking me all the time in the face, placed a large diamond on my finger, saying something about its being from the land to which he was going. I refused to take it, for I had heard that the Emperor died poor. But as he begged me to keep it, at least till he should come back, it has hardly left my hand since he placed it there.

Piteous that this heir to the throne of France should die alone in the yellow grass at the hand of savages in that same land where the great Emperor had said: "Soldiers, from yonder pyramids twenty centuries behold your deeds."

Dead ! Dead ! stark in the long, strong grass !
He died with his sword in his hand.
Who says it ? who saw it ? God saw it !
And I knew him ! St. George ! he would draw it,
Though they swooped down in mass
Till they darkened the land !
Then the seventeen wounds in his breast !
Ah ! these witness best.

Dead ! Stark dead in the long, strong grass !
Dead ! and alone in the great dark land !
O mother ! not Empress now, mother !
A nobler name, too, than all other,

The laurel leaf fades from thy hand !
O mother that waiteth, a mass !
Masses and chants must be said,
And cypress, instead.

MY LAST DAY WITH MR. LONGFELLOW.

Many others, I know, stood nearer him, so much nearer and dearer, and maybe I ought not to claim the right to say much of a sacred nature; but somehow I always felt, when he reached out his right hand and drew me to him, and looked me fairly and silently in the face with his earnest seer eyes, that he knew me, did not dislike me, and that he knew, soul to soul, we sought the good and the beautiful and true, each after his fashion, and as best he knew.

He had a pretty way of always getting out of the house—that beautiful house of his, where Washington had dwelt—into the woods. He possessed a wonderful lot of books, but he knew the birds, the crickets, the flowers, woods and grasses were more in my way, and with rare delicacy he never talked on books at all, but led out at once, whenever possible, to our mutual friends in the rear of the old Headquarters of Washington.

Walt Whitman chanced to be in Boston when I last visited Mr. Longfellow, and I was delighted to hear the poet at his table in the midst of his perfect family speak of him most kindly. Soon after he looked me up at my hotel in Boston, and we two called on the good, gray poet together. I mention this merely to italicize the suggestion that Longfellow's was a large nature.

It was on this occasion that a pall of black suddenly fell upon the Republic. Garfield lay dead at Elberon!

A publisher solicited from each of the several authors then in and about Boston some tribute of sorrow for the dead. The generous sum of $100 was checked as an earnest. I remember how big-hearted John Boyle O'Reilly and I got Walt Whitman down in a cave somewhere under the Revere House, where a bottle of champagne was found, and wrestled with him in a vain effort to make him earn and accept his $100.

"Yes, I'm sorry as the sorriest; sympathize with the great broken heart of the world over this dead sovereign citizen. But I've nothing to say."

And so, persuade as we might, even till past midnight, Walt Whitman would not touch the money or try to write a line. He was poor; but bear it forever in testimony that he was honest, and would not promise to sell that which he felt that God had not at that moment given him to sell. And hereafter, whenever any of you are disposed to speak or even think unkindly of Walt Whitman, remember this refusal of his to touch a whole heap of money when he might have had it for ten lines, and maybe less than ten minutes' employment. I love him for it. There is not a butcher, nor a baker, nor a merchant, not a banker in America, perhaps, who would have been, under the circumstances, so stubbornly, savagely honest with the world and himself.

O'Reilly had already written his glorious lines, and was happy. He paid for the champagne, I think. Memory is a little confused here. But I know that is a way he has. Soon after midnight I left the others in the cave, and went up to my room in the hotel and went to work. Early next morning I drove over to Mr. Longfellow in great haste and read my lines. Kindly he listened as I read, and then carefully looked them all over and made some important improvements. He had also partly written, and read me, his poem on the sad theme. But it was too stately and fine for company with our less mature work, and at the last moment it was withheld on the plea that it was still incomplete. It soon after appeared in the New York *Independent*. As I was hastening away with my manuscript for the press, he said as he came with me down to the gate, that the Queen of England had done more to conquer America by sending the wreath for the funeral of the dead President than all the Georges had ever done with all their troops and cannon. And he said it in such a poetical way that I thought it an unfinished couplet of his poem. I never saw him any more.

GARFIELD.

"Bear me out of the battle, for lo, I am sorely wounded."

From out the vast, wide-bosomed West,
    Where gnarled old maples make array,
Deep scarred from Redmen gone to rest,
    Where unnamed heroes hew the way
For worlds to follow in their quest;
    Where pipes the quail, where squirrels play
Through tops of trees with nuts for toy,
    A boy stood forth clear-eyed and tall,
A timid boy, a bashful boy,
    Yet comely as the sons of Saul—
A boy all friendless, all unknown,
Yet heir-apparent to a throne:

A throne the proudest ever known
    For him who bears him noblest, best,
And it was won by him alone,
    That boy from out that wooded West.
And now to fall! Pale-browed and prone
    He lies in everlasting rest,

The nations clasp the cold, dead hand;
    The nations sob aloud at this;
The only dry eyes in the line
    Now at the last we know are his,
While she who sends a wreath has won
More conquest than her hosts had done.

Brave heart, farewell. The wheel has run
    Full circle, and behold a grave
Beneath the old loved trees is done.
    The druid oaks lift up and wave
    A solemn beckon back. The brave
Old maples welcome every one.
    Receive him, earth. In center land,
As in the center of each heart,
    As in the hollow of God's hand,
The coffin sinks. And we depart
Each on his way, as God deems best
To *do*, and so deserve to rest.

TO MOUNT SHASTA.

I stood where thunderbolts were wont
To smite thy Titan-fashioned front;
I heard huge mountains rock and roll;
  I saw the lightning's gleaming rod
Reach forth and write on heaven's scroll
  The awful autograph of God!

FINALE.

When ye have conned the hundreth time
   My sins and sagely magnified
Your oft-told fictions into crimes
   Dark planned, and so turned all aside,
Why then have done, I beg, I pray.
   These shadows ye have fashioned lie
So heavily along my way.
   And I would fain have light :   And I
Would fain have love :   Have love one little hour
   Ere God has plucked my day, a tearful flower.

But when the cloud-draped day is done,
   Now happily not long for me,
For lo ! I see no more the sun,
   Say this, if say ye must, and see
That ye mouth not the simple truth
   "From first to last this man had naught
Of us but insolence. From youth
   Right on, alone he silent wrought
Nor answered us. And yet from us he knew
   But thrust of lance that thrust him through and
      through."

Ah me! I mind me long agone,
   Once on a savage snow-bound height
We pigmies pierced a king. Upon
   His bare and upreared breast till night
We rained red arrows and we rained
   Hot lead. Then up the steep and slow
He passed; yet ever still disdained
   To strike, or even look below.
We found the grizzly high 'mid clouds next morn
   And dead, in all his silent, splendid scorn.

So leave me, as the edge of night
   Comes on a little time to pass,
Or pray. For steep the stony height
   And torn by storm, and bare of grass
Or blossom. And when I lie dead
   Oh, do not drag me down once more.
For Jesus' sake let my poor head
   Lie pillowed 'mid these stones. My store
Of wealth is these. I earned them. Let me keep
   Still on alone, on mine own star-lit steep.

The gift of song is, to my mind, a solemn gift. The prophet and the seer should rise above the levities of this life. And so it is that I make humble apology for now gathering up from recitation books these last pages. The only excuse for doing it is their refusal to die; even under the mutilations of the compilers of "choice selections."

IN CLASSIC SHADES.

ALONE and sad I sat me down
To rest on Rousseau's narrow isle
Below Geneva. Mile on mile,
And set with many a shining town,
Tow'rd Dent du Midi danced the wave
Beneath the moon. Winds went and came
And fanned the stars into a flame.
I heard the far lake, dark and deep,
Rise up and talk as in its sleep;
I heard the laughing waters lave
And lap against the further shore,
An idle oar, and nothing more
Save that the isle had voice, and save
That 'round about its base of stone
There plashed and flashed the foamy Rhone.

A stately man, as black as tan,
Kept up a stern and broken round
Among the strangers on the ground.
I named that awful African
A second Hannibal.

.

                    I gat
My elbows on the table ; sat
With chin in upturned palm to scan
His face, and contemplate the scene.
The moon rode by a crownèd queen.
I was alone. Lo! not a man
To speak my mother tongue. Ah me!
How more than all alone can be
A man in crowds! Across the isle
My Hannibal strode on. The while
Diminished Rousseau sat his throne
Of books, unnoticed and unknown.

This strange, strong man, with face austere,
At last drew near. He bowed ; he spake
In unknown tongues. I could but shake
My head. Then half achill with fear,
I rose, and sought another place.
Again I mused. The kings of thought
Came by, and on that storied spot
I lifted up a tearful face.
The star-set Alps they sang a tune
Unheard by any soul but mine.
Mont Blanc, as lone and as divine
And white, seemed mated to the moon.
The past was mine ; strong-voiced and vast—

Stern Calvin, strange Voltaire, and Tell,
And two whose names are known too well
To name, in grand procession passed.

And yet again came Hannibal;
King-like he came, and drawing near,
I saw his brow was now severe
And resolute.

          In tongues unknown
Again he spake. I was alone,
Was all unarmed, was worn and sad;
But now, at last, my spirit had
Its old assertion.

          I arose,
As startled from a dull repose;
With gathered strength I raised a hand
And cried, "I do not understand."

His black face brightened as I spake;
He bowed; he wagged his woolly head;
He showed his shining teeth, and said,
"Sah, if you please, dose tables heah
Am consecrate to lager beer;
And, sah, what will you have to take?"

Not that I loved that colored cuss—
Nay! he had awed me all too much—
But I sprang forth, and with a clutch
I grasped his hand, and holding thus,
Cried, "Bring my country's drink for two!"
For oh! that speech of Saxon sound
To me was as a fountain found
In wastes, and thrilled me through and through.

*   *   *   *   *

On Rousseau's isle, in Rousseau's shade,
Two pink and spicy drinks were made;
In classic shades, on classic ground,
We stirred two cocktails round and round.

THAT GENTLE MAN FROM BOSTON TOWN.

AN IDYL OF OREGON.

Two webfoot brothers loved a fair
   Young lady, rich and good to see ;
And oh, her black abundant hair !
   And oh, her wondrous witchery !
Her father kept a cattle farm,
These brothers kept her safe from harm :

From harm of cattle on the hill ;
   From thick-necked bulls loud bellowing
The livelong morning, loud and shrill,
   And lashing sides like anything !
From roaring bulls that tossed the sand
And pawed the lilies from the land.

There came a third young man. He came
   From far and famous Boston town.
He was not handsome, was not "game,"
   But he could "cook a goose" as brown
As any man that set foot on
The sunlit shores of Oregon.

This Boston man he taught the school,
   Taught gentleness and love alway,
Said love and kindness, as a rule,
   Would ultimately "make it pay."
He was so gentle, kind, that he
Could make a noun and verb agree.

So when one day the brothers grew
   All jealous and did strip to fight,
He gently stood between the two
   And meekly told them 'twas not right.
"I have a higher, better plan,"
Outspake this gentle Boston man.

"My plan is this : Forget this fray
   About that lily hand of hers ;
Go take your guns and hunt all day
   High up yon lofty hill of firs,
And while you hunt, my loving doves,
Why, I will learn which one she loves."

The brothers sat the windy hill,
   Their hair shone yellow, like spun gold,
Their rifles crossed their laps, but still
   They sat and sighed and shook with cold.
Their hearts lay bleeding far below ;
Above them gleamed white peaks of snow.

Their hounds lay couching, slim and neat,
   A spotted circle in the grass.
The valley lay beneath their feet;
   They heard the wide-winged eagles pass.
The eagles cleft the clouds above;
Yet what could they but sigh and love?

"If I could die," the elder sighed,
   "My dear young brother here might wed."
"Oh, would to heaven I had died!"
   The younger sighed with bended head.
Then each looked each full in the face
And each sprang up and stood in place.

"If I could die" — the elder spake,—
   "Die by your hand, the world would say
'T was accident —; and for her sake,
   Dear brother, be it so, I pray."
"Not that!" the younger nobly said;
Then tossed his gun and turned his head.

And fifty paces back he paced!
   And as he paced he drew the ball;
Then sudden stopped and wheeled and faced
   His brother to the death and fall!
Two shots rang wild upon the air!
But lo! the two stood harmless there!

An eagle poised high in the air ;
    Far, far below the bellowing
Of bullocks ceased, and everywhere
    Vast silence sat all questioning.
The spotted hounds ran circling round,
Their red, wet noses to the ground.

And now each brother came to know
    That each had drawn the deadly ball ;
And for that fair girl far below
    Had sought in vain to silent fall.
And then the two did gladly " shake "
And thus the elder bravely spake :

" Now let us run right hastily
    And tell the kind schoolmaster all !
Yea ! yea ! and if she choose not me,
    But all on you her favors fall,
This valiant scene, till all life ends,
Dear brother, binds us best of friends."

The hounds sped down, a spotted line,
    The bulls in tall abundant grass
Shook back their horns from bloom and vine,
    And trumpeted to see them pass —
They loved so good, they loved so true,
These brothers scarce knew what to do.

They sought the kind schoolmaster out
   As swift as sweeps the light of morn —
They could but love, they could not doubt
   This man so gentle, "in a horn."
They cried : " Now whose the lily hand —
That lady's of this webfoot land ? "

They bowed before that big-nosed man,
   That long-nosed man from Boston town ;
They talked as only lovers can,
   They talked, but he could only frown ;
And still they talked and still they plead ;
It was as pleading with the dead.

At last this Boston man did speak —
   " Her father has a thousand ceows,
An hundred bulls, all fat and sleek ;
   He also had this ample heouse."
The brothers' eyes stuck out thereat
So far you might have hung your hat.

" I liked the looks of this big heouse —
   My lovely boys, won't you come in ?
Her father has a thousand ceows,
   He also had a heap of tin.
The guirl ? Oh yes, the guirl, you see —
The guirl, just neow she married me."

WILLIAM BROWN OF OREGON.

They called him Bill, the hired man,
   But she, her name was Mary Jane,
   The squire's daughter; and to reign
The belle from Ber-she-be to Dan
Her little game. How lovers rash
   Got mittens at the spelling school!
   How many a mute, inglorious fool
Wrote rhymes and sighed and dyed—mustache!

This hired man had loved her long,
   Had loved her best and first and last,
   Her very garments as she passed
For him had symphony and song.
So when one day with sudden frown
   She called him "Bill," he raised his head,
   He caught her eye and faltering said,
"I love you; and my name is Brown."

She fairly waltzed with rage; she wept;
   You would have thought the house on fire.
   She told her sire, the portly squire,
Then smelt her smelling-salts and slept.

Poor William did what could be done ;
    He swung a pistol on each hip,
    He gathered up a great ox-whip
And drove toward the setting sun.

He crossed the great backbone of earth,
    He saw the snowy mountains rolled
    Like mighty billows; saw the gold
Of awful sunsets; felt the birth
Of sudden dawn that burst the night
    Like resurrection; saw the face
    Of God and named it boundless space
Ringed round with room and shoreless light.

Her lovers passed. Wolves hunt in packs,
    They sought for bigger game; somehow
    They seemed to see above her brow
The forky sign of turkey tracks.
The teter-board of life goes up,
    The teter-board of life goes down,
    The sweetest face must learn to frown;
The biggest dog has been a pup.

O maidens! pluck not at the air;
    The sweetest flowers I have found
    Grow rather close unto the ground
And highest places are most bare.

Why, you had better win the grace
   Of one poor cussed Af-ri-can
   Than win the eyes of every man
In love alone with his own face.

At last she nursed her true desire.
   She sighed, she wept for William Brown.
   She watched the splendid sun go down
Like some great sailing ship on fire,
Then rose and checked her trunk right on;
   And in the cars she lunched and lunched,
   And had her ticket punched and punched,
Until she came to Oregon.

She reached the limit of the lines,
   She wore blue specs upon her nose,
   Wore rather short and manly clothes,
And so set out to reach the mines.
Her pocket held a parasol,
   Her right hand held a Testament,
   And thus equipped right on she went,
Went water-proof and water-fall.

She saw a miner gazing down,
   Slow stirring something with a spoon;
   "O, tell me true and tell me soon,
What has become of William Brown?"

He looked askance beneath her specs,
   Then stirred his cocktail round and round,
   Then raised his head and sighed profound,
And said, "He's handed in his checks."

Then care fed on her damaged cheek,
   And she grew faint, did Mary Jane,
   And smelt her smelling-salts in vain,
And wandered, weary, worn and weak.
At last, upon a hill alone,
   She came, and there she sat her down;
   For on that hill there stood a stone,
And, lo! that stone read, "William Brown."

"O William Brown! O William Brown!
   And here you rest at last," she said,
   "With this lone stone above your head,
And forty miles from any town!
I will plant cypress trees, I will,
   And I will build a fence around,
   And I will fertilize the ground
With tears enough to turn a mill."

She went and got a hired man,
   She brought him forty miles from town,
   And in the tall grass squatted down
And bade him build as she should plan.

But cruel cowboys with their bands
  They saw, and hurriedly they ran
  And told a bearded cattle man
Somebody builded on his lands.

He took his rifle from the rack,
  He girt himself in battle pelt,
  He stuck two pistols in his belt,
And mounting on his horse's back,
He plunged ahead. But when they showed
  A woman fair, about his eyes
  He pulled his hat, and he likewise
Pulled at his beard, and chewed and chewed.

At last he gat him down and spake;
  "O lady dear, what do you here?"
  "I build a tomb unto my dear,
I plant sweet flowers for his sake."
The bearded man threw his two hands
  Above his head, then brought them down
  And cried, "O, I am William Brown,
And this the corner-stone of my lands!"

HORACE GREELEY'S DRIVE.

The old stage-drivers of the brave old days!
  The old stage-drivers with their dash and trust!
These old stage-drivers they have gone their ways,
  But their deeds live on, though their bones are dust;
And many a tale is told and retold
Of these daring men in the days of old:

Of honest Hank Monk and his Tally-Ho,
  When he took good Horace in his stage to climb
The high Sierras with their peaks of snow
  And 'cross to Nevada, "and come in on time;"
But the canyon below was so deep—oh! so deep—
And the summit above was so steep—oh! so steep!

The horses were foaming. The summit ahead
  Seemed as far as the stars on a still, clear night.
And steeper and steeper the narrow route led
  Till up to the peaks of perpetual white;
But the faithful Hank Monk, with his face to the snow,
Sat silent and stern on his Tally-Ho!

Sat silent and still, sat faithful and true
   To the great, good man in his charge that day;
Sat vowing the man and the mail should "go through
   On time" though he bursted both brace and stay;
Sat silently vowing, in face of the snow,
He'd "get in on time" with his Tally-Ho!

But the way was so steep and so slow—oh! so slow!
   'T was silver below, and the bright silver peaks
Were silver above in their beauty of snow,
   Where eagles swooped by, with their bright, shiny beaks;
When, sudden out-popping a head snowy white—
"Mr. Monk, I *must* lecture in Nevada to-night!"

With just one thought that the mail must go through;
   With just one word to the great, good man—
But weary—so weary—the creaking stage drew
   As only a weary old creaking stage can—
When again shot the head; came shrieking outright;
"Mr. Monk, I MUST lecture in Nevada to-night!"

Just then came the summit! And the wide world below.
   It was Hank Monk's world. But he no word spake;
He pushed back his hat to that high peak of snow!
   He threw out his foot to the great strong brake!

He threw out his silk!   He threw out his reins!
And the great wheels reeled as if reeling snow skeins!

The eagles were lost in their crags up above!
  The horses flew swift as the swift light of morn!
The mail must go through with its message of love,
  The miners were waiting his bright bugle horn.
The *man* must go through!   And Monk made a vow
As he never had failed, why, he would n't fail now!

How his stage spun the peak like a fair spider's web!
  It was spider and fly in the heavens up there!
And the swift swirling wheels made the blood flow
    and ebb,
  For 'twas death in the breadth of a wheel or a
    hair.
Once more popped the head, and the piping voice
    cried:
"Mr. Monk!   Mr. Monk!"   But no Monk replied!

Then the great stage it swung, as if swung from the
    sky;
  Then it dipped like a ship in the deep jaws of death;
Then the good man he gasped as men gasping for
    breath,
  When they deem it is coming their hour to die.

And again shot the head, like a battering ram,
   And the face it was red, and the words they
      hot :
"Mr. Monk! Mr. Monk! I don't care a ——
   Whether I lecture in Nevada or not!"

THAT FAITHFUL WIFE OF IDAHO.

Huge silver snow-peaks, white as wool,
   Huge, sleek, fat steers knee-deep in grass,
And belly deep, and belly full,
   Their flower-beds one fragrant mass.
Oh, flower land so calmly grand,
   Where flowers chase the flying snow!
Oh, high-held land in God's right hand,
   Delicious, dreamful Idaho!

We rode the rolling cow-sown hills,
   That bearded cattle man and I;
Below us laughed the blossomed rills,
   Above the dappled clouds blew by.
We talked. The topic? Guess. Why, sir,
   Three-fourths of all men's time they keep
To talk, to think, to *be* of HER;
   The other fourth they give to sleep.

To learn what he might know of love,
   I laughed all constancy to scorn.
"Behold yon happy, changeful dove!
   Behold this day, all storm at morn,

Yet now 't is changed by cloud and sun,
  Yea, all things change—the heart, the head,
Behold on earth there is not one
  That changeth not in love," I said.

He drew a glass, as if to scan
  The steeps for steers; raised it and sighed.
He craned his neck, this cattle man,
  Then drove the cork home and replied:
"For twenty years (forgive these tears),
  For twenty years no word of strife—
I have not known for twenty years
  One folly from my faithful wife."

I looked that tarn man in the face—
  That dark-browed, bearded cattle man.
He pulled his beard, then dropped in place
  A broad right hand, all scarred and tan,
And toyed with something shining there
  Above his holster, bright and small.
I was convinced. I did not care
  To agitate his mind at all.

But rest I could not. Know I must
  The story of my stalwart guide;
His dauntless love, enduring trust;
  His blessed and most immortal bride.

I wondered, marveled, marveled much ;
   Was she of Western growth ? Was she
Of Saxon blood, that wife with such
   Eternal truth and constancy ?

I could not rest until I knew —
   " Now twenty years, my man," said I,
" Is a long time." He turned, he drew
   A pistol forth, also a sigh.
" 'T is twenty years or more," sighed he.
   " Nay, nay, my honest man, I vow
I do not doubt that this may be ;
   But tell, oh ! tell me truly how ?"

" 'T would make a poem, pure and grand ;
   All time should note it near and far ;
And thy fair, virgin, gold-sown land
   Should stand out like a winter star.
America should heed. And then
   The doubtful French beyond the sea —
'T would make them truer, nobler men
   To know how this might truly be."

" 'T is twenty years or more," urged he ;
   " Nay, that I know, good guide of mine ;
But lead me where this wife may be,
   And I a pilgrim at a shrine,

And kneeling as a pilgrim true " —
   He, leaning, shouted loud and clear :
" I can not show my wife to you ;
   She 's dead this more than twenty year."

SARATOGA AND THE PSALMIST.

These famous waters smell like—well,
   Those Saratoga waters may
   Taste just a little of the day
Of judgment; and the sulphur smell
   Suggests, along with other things,
   A climate rather warm for springs.

But restful as a twilight song,
   The land where every lover hath
   A spring, and every spring a path
To lead love pleasantly along,
   Oh, there be waters, not of springs—
   The waters wise King David sings.

Sweet is the bread that lovers eat
   In secret, sang on harp of gold,
   Jerusalem's high king of old.
"The stolen waters they are sweet!"
   Oh, dear, delicious piracies
   Of kisses upon love's high seas!

The old traditions of our race
    Repeat for aye and still repeat;
    The stolen waters still are sweet
As when King David sat in place,
    All purple robed and crowned in gold,
    And sang his holy psalms of old.

Oh, to escape the scorching sun;
    To seek these waters ever sweet;
    To see her dip her dimpled feet
Where these delicious waters run—
    To dip her feet, nor slip nor fall,
    Nor stain her garment's hem at all;

Nor soil the whiteness of her feet,
    Nor stain her whitest garment's hem—
    Oh, singer of Jerusalem,
You sang so sweet, so wisely sweet!
    Shake hands! shake hands! I guess you knew
    For all your psalms, a thing or two.

FINIS.

www.ingramcontent.com/pod-product-compliance
Lightning Source LLC
Chambersburg PA
CBHW030348170426
43202CB00010B/1294